CROCK·POT®

◆ THE ORIGINAL SLOW COOKER ◆

Quick & Easy
Recipes

Publications International, Ltd.

Pictured on the front cover: Parsnip and Carrot Soup *(page 70)*.
Pictured on the back cover (clockwise from top): Caponata *(page 6)*, New England Clam Chowder *(page 54)*, Hot Fudge Cake *(page 88)* and Mama's Beer Chili *(page 64)*.

table of contents

hints & tips

Slow Cooker Sizes

Smaller slow cookers, such as 1- to 3½-quart models, are the perfect size for singles, a couple, empty-nesters and also for serving dips.

While medium size slow cookers (those holding somewhere between 3 quarts and 5 quarts) will easily cook enough food at a time to feed a small family, they are also convenient for holiday side dishes or appetizers.

Large slow cookers are great for large family dinners, holiday entertaining and potluck suppers. A 6- to 7-quart model is ideal if you like to make meals in advance and have dinner tonight and store leftovers for another day.

Types of Slow Cookers

Current models of **CROCK-POT®** slow cookers come equipped with many different features and benefits, from auto cook programs, to stovetop-safe stoneware to timed programming. Visit **www.crockpot.com** to find the slow cooker that best suits your needs and lifestyle.

Cooking, Stirring and Food Safety

CROCK-POT® slow cookers are safe to leave unattended. The outer heating base may get hot as it cooks, but it should not pose a fire hazard The heating element in the heating base functions at a low wattage and is safe for your countertops.

Your slow cooker should be filled about one-half to three-fourths full for most recipes unless otherwise instructed. Lean meats such as chicken or pork tenderloin will cook faster than meats with more connective tissue and fat such as beef chuck or pork shoulder. Bone-in meats will take longer than boneless cuts. Typical slow cooker dishes take approximately 7 to 8 hours to reach the simmer point on LOW and about 3 to 4 hours on HIGH. Once the vegetables and meat start to simmer and braise, their flavors will fully blend and meat will become fall-off-the bone tender.

According to the USDA, all bacteria are killed at a temperature of 165°F. If you need to open the lid to check on your food or are adding additional ingredients, remember to allow additional cooking time if necessary to ensure food is cooked through and tender.

Large slow cookers, the 6- to 7-quart sizes, may benefit with a quick stir halfway during cook time to help distribute heat and promote even cooking. It is usually unnecessary to stir at all as even ½ cup liquid will help to distribute heat and the crockery is the perfect medium for holding food at an even temperature throughout the cooking process.

Oven-Safe

All **CROCK-POT**® slow cooker removable crockery inserts may (without their lids) be used in ovens at up to 400°F safely. Also, all **CROCK-POT**® slow cookers are microwavable without their lids. If you own another brand slow cooker, please refer to your owner's manual for specific crockery cooking medium tolerances.

Frozen Food

Frozen food or partially frozen food can be successfully cooked in a slow cooker, however it will require longer cooking than the same recipe made with fresh food. Using an instant read thermometer is recommended to ensure meat is fully cooked through.

Pasta and Rice

If you are converting a recipe that calls for uncooked pasta, cook them on the stovetop just until slightly tender before adding to slow cooker. If you are converting a recipe that calls for cooked rice, stir in raw rice with other ingredients; add ¼ cup extra liquid per ¼ cup of raw rice.

Beans

Beans must be softened completely before combining with sugar and/or acidic foods. Sugar and acid have a hardening effect on beans and will prevent softening. Fully cooked canned beans may be used as a substitute for dried beans.

Vegetables

Root vegetables often cook more slowly than meat. Cut vegetables accordingly to cook at the same rate as meat, large or small, or lean versus marbled, and place near the sides or bottom of the stoneware to facilitate cooking.

Herbs

Fresh herbs add flavor and color when added at the end of the cooking cycle but for dishes with shorter cook times, hearty, fresh herbs such as rosemary and thyme hold up well. If added at the beginning, many fresh herbs' flavor will dissipate over long cook times. Ground and/or dried herbs and spices work well in slow cooking and may be added at the beginning. The flavor power of all herbs and spices can vary greatly depending on their particular strength and shelf life. Use chili powders and garlic powder sparingly as these can sometimes intensify over the long cook times. Always taste dish at end of cook cycle and correct seasonings including salt and pepper.

Liquids

It is not necessary to use more than ½ to 1 cup liquid in most instances since juices in meats and vegetables are retained more in slow cooking than in conventional cooking. Excess liquid can be cooked down and concentrated after slow cooking on the stovetop or by removing meat and vegetables from stoneware, stirring in cornstarch or tapioca and setting the slow cooker to HIGH. Cook on HIGH for approximately 15 minutes until juices are thickened.

Milk

Milk, cream, and sour cream break down during extended cooking. When possible, add during last 15 to 30 minutes of cooking, until just heated through. Condensed soups may be substituted for milk and can cook for extended times.

Fish

Fish is delicate and should be stirred in gently during the last 15 to 30 minutes of cooking time. Cook until just cooked through and serve immediately.

starters

Caponata

- 1 medium eggplant (about 1 pound), peeled and cut into ½-inch pieces
- 1 can (14½ ounces) diced Italian plum tomatoes, undrained
- 1 medium onion, chopped
- 1 red bell pepper, cut into ½-inch pieces
- ½ cup medium-hot salsa
- ¼ cup extra-virgin olive oil
- 2 tablespoons capers, drained
- 2 tablespoons balsamic vinegar
- 3 cloves garlic, minced
- 1 teaspoon dried oregano
- ¼ teaspoon salt
- ⅓ cup packed fresh basil, cut into thin strips
- Toasted sliced Italian or French bread

1. Mix eggplant, tomatoes, onion, bell pepper, salsa, oil, capers, vinegar, garlic, oregano and salt in **CROCK-POT®** slow cooker.

2. Cover; cook on LOW 7 to 8 hours or until vegetables are crisp-tender.

3. Stir in basil. Serve at room temperature on toasted bread.

Makes about 5¼ cups

Pizza Fondue

½ pound bulk Italian sausage

1 cup chopped onion

2 jars (26 ounces each) meatless pasta sauce

4 ounces thinly sliced ham, finely chopped

1 package (3 ounces) sliced pepperoni, finely chopped

¼ teaspoon red pepper flakes

1 pound mozzarella cheese, cut into ¾-inch cubes

1 loaf Italian or French bread, cut into 1-inch cubes

1. Cook and stir sausage and onion in large skillet over medium-high heat until sausage is browned. Drain and discard fat.

2. Transfer sausage mixture to **CROCK-POT®** slow cooker. Stir in pasta sauce, ham, pepperoni and pepper flakes. Cover; cook on LOW 3 to 4 hours. Serve warm fondue with mozzarella cheese and bread cubes.

Makes 20 to 25 appetizer servings

Warm Blue Crab Bruschetta

4 cups peeled, seeded and diced Roma or plum tomatoes

1 cup diced white onion

2 teaspoons minced garlic

⅓ cup olive oil

2 tablespoons balsamic vinegar

½ teaspoon dried oregano

2 tablespoons sugar

1 pound lump blue crabmeat, picked over for shells

1½ teaspoons kosher salt

½ teaspoon cracked black pepper

⅓ cup minced fresh basil

2 baguettes, sliced and toasted

1. Combine tomatoes, onion, garlic, oil, vinegar, oregano and sugar in **CROCK-POT®** slow cooker. Cover; cook on LOW 2 hours.

2. Add crabmeat, salt and pepper. Stir gently to mix, taking care not to break up crabmeat lumps. Cook on LOW 1 hour.

3. Fold in basil. Serve on toasted baguette slices.

Makes 16 servings

Serving Suggestion: Crab topping can also be served on Melba toast or whole-grain crackers.

Slow Cooker Cheese Dip

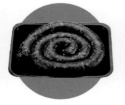   

1 pound 95% lean ground beef
1 pound bulk Italian sausage
1 package (16 ounces) pasteurized processed cheese spread, cubed
1 can (11 ounces) sliced jalapeño peppers, drained*
1 medium onion, diced
8 ounces Cheddar cheese, cubed
1 package (8 ounces) cream cheese, cubed
1 container (8 ounces) cottage cheese
1 container (8 ounces) sour cream
1 can (8 ounces) diced tomatoes, drained
3 cloves garlic, minced
Salt and pepper, to taste

*Jalapeño peppers can sting and irritate the skin, so wear rubber gloves when handling peppers and do not touch eyes.

1. Brown ground beef and sausage in medium skillet over medium-high heat, stirring to break up meat. Drain and discard fat. Transfer to **CROCK-POT®** slow cooker.

2. Add processed cheese, jalapeño peppers, onion, Cheddar cheese, cream cheese, cottage cheese, sour cream, tomatoes and garlic to **CROCK-POT®** slow cooker. Season with salt and pepper.

3. Cover; cook on HIGH 1½ to 2 hours or until cheeses are melted. Serve with crackers or tortilla chips.

Makes 16 to 18 servings

Tip: For a lower fat version of this recipe, use reduced-fat Cheddar cheese and Neufchâtel cheese instead of full-fat cream cheese.

Asian-Spiced Chicken Wings

3 pounds chicken wings

1 cup packed brown sugar

1 cup soy sauce

½ cup ketchup

2 teaspoons fresh ginger, minced

2 cloves garlic, minced

¼ cup dry sherry

½ cup hoisin sauce

1 tablespoon fresh lime juice

3 tablespoons sesame seeds, toasted

¼ cup green onions, thinly sliced

1. Broil the chicken wings 10 minutes on each side or until browned. Transfer chicken wings to **CROCK-POT®** slow cooker. Add remaining ingredients, except hoisin sauce, lime juice, sesame seeds and green onions; stir thoroughly. Cover; cook on LOW 5 to 6 hours or on HIGH 2 to 3 hours or until wings are no longer pink, stirring once halfway through the cooking time to baste the wings with sauce.

2. Remove wings from **CROCK-POT®** slow cooker. Remove ¼ cup of cooking liquid (discard the rest). Combine liquid with hoisin sauce and lime juice. Drizzle mixture over wings.

3. Before serving, sprinkle wings with sesame seeds and green onions.

Makes 10 to 16 wings

Note: Chicken wings are always crowd pleasers. Garnishing them with toasted sesame seeds and green onions gives these appetizers added crunch and contrasting color.

Tip: For 5-, 6- or 7-quart **CROCK-POT®** *slow cooker, increase chicken wings to 5 pounds.*

Honey-Sauced Chicken Wings

3 pounds chicken wings

1 teaspoon salt

½ teaspoon black pepper

1 cup honey

½ cup soy sauce

¼ cup chopped onion

¼ cup ketchup

2 tablespoons vegetable oil

2 cloves garlic, minced

¼ teaspoon red pepper flakes

Toasted sesame seeds (optional)

1. Preheat broiler. Cut off and discard chicken wing tips. Cut each wing at joint to make 2 sections. Sprinkle wing parts with salt and pepper. Place on broiler pan. Broil 4 to 5 inches from heat about 10 minutes per side, or until chicken wings are brown. Transfer to **CROCK-POT®** slow cooker.

2. For sauce, combine honey, soy sauce, onion, ketchup, oil, garlic and pepper flakes in bowl. Pour over chicken wings.

3. Cover; cook on LOW 4 to 5 hours or on HIGH 2 to 2½ hours. Garnish with sesame seeds, if desired.

Makes 24 to 32 appetizers

Cocktail Meatballs

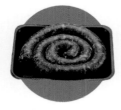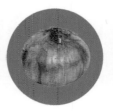

1 **pound 95% lean ground beef**

1 **pound bulk pork or Italian sausage**

1 **cup cracker crumbs**

1 **cup finely chopped onion**

1 **cup finely chopped green bell pepper**

½ **cup milk**

1 **egg, beaten**

2 **teaspoons salt**

1 **teaspoon dried Italian seasoning**

¼ **teaspoon black pepper**

1 **cup ketchup**

¾ **cup packed dark brown sugar**

½ **cup (1 stick) butter or margarine**

½ **cup vinegar**

¼ **cup lemon juice**

¼ **cup water**

1 **teaspoon prepared mustard**

¼ **teaspoon garlic salt**

1. Preheat oven to 350°F. Combine beef, pork, cracker crumbs, onion, bell pepper, milk, egg, salt, Italian seasoning and pepper in bowl. Mix well; form into 1-inch meatballs. Place meatballs onto 2 nonstick baking sheets. Bake 25 minutes or until browned.

2. Meanwhile, place ketchup, sugar, butter, vinegar, lemon juice, water, mustard and garlic salt into **CROCK-POT®** slow cooker; mix well. Cover; cook on HIGH 15 to 20 minutes or until hot.

3. Transfer meatballs to **CROCK-POT®** slow cooker; carefully stir to coat with sauce. Reduce heat to LOW. Cover; cook 2 hours.

Makes about 24 meatballs

beef

Roast Beef Burritos

- 1 boneless beef rump or bottom round roast (3 to 5 pounds)
- ¼ cup water
- ½ to 1 teaspoon garlic powder
- ½ to 1 teaspoon black pepper
- 1 bay leaf
- 2 jars (16 ounces each) salsa, plus extra for garnish
- 2 cans (4 ounces each) diced green chiles, undrained
- ½ large yellow onion, diced
- 8 to 10 burrito-size flour tortillas
- 1 cup shredded Cheddar cheese

1. Place roast in **CROCK-POT®** slow cooker; add water. Season with garlic powder and pepper to taste. Add bay leaf. Cover; cook on HIGH 6 hours or until beef is tender. Remove bay leaf and discard.

2. Transfer beef to cutting board. Trim fat from beef and discard. Shred beef with two forks. Let cooking liquid stand 5 minutes to allow fat to rise. Skim off fat and discard. Add shredded beef, salsa, chiles and onion to cooking liquid in **CROCK-POT®** slow cooker; stir to combine. Cover; cook on HIGH 1 hour or until onion is tender.

3. To serve, place about 3 tablespoons beef onto each tortilla. Top with cheese and fold into burritos. Place burrito, seam side down, on plate. Microwave 30 seconds to melt cheese. Serve with extra salsa, if desired.

Makes 8 to 10 servings

Philly Cheese Steaks

2 pounds round steak, sliced

2 tablespoons butter or margarine, melted

4 onions, sliced

2 green bell peppers, sliced

1 tablespoon garlic-pepper blend

Salt, to taste

½ cup water

2 teaspoons beef bouillon granules

8 crusty Italian or French rolls*

8 slices Cheddar cheese, cut in half

*Toast rolls on griddle or under broiler, if desired.

1. Combine steak, butter, onions, green pepper, garlic-pepper blend and salt in **CROCK-POT®** slow cooker; stir to mix.

2. Whisk together water and bouillon in small bowl; pour into **CROCK-POT®** slow cooker. Cover; cook on LOW 6 to 8 hours.

3. Remove meat, onions and bell pepper from **CROCK-POT®** slow cooker and pile on rolls. Top with cheese and place under broiler until cheese is melted.

Makes 8 servings

Slow-Cooked Pot Roast

1 tablespoon vegetable oil

1 beef brisket (3 to 4 pounds)

1 tablespoon garlic powder, divided

1 tablespoon salt, divided

1 tablespoon black pepper, divided

1 teaspoon paprika, divided

5 to 6 new potatoes, cut into quarters

4 to 5 medium onions, sliced

1 pound baby carrots

1 can (14½ ounces) beef broth

1. Heat oil on HIGH in **CROCK-POT**® slow cooker. Brown brisket on all sides. Transfer brisket to plate. Season with 1½ teaspoons garlic powder, 1½ teaspoons salt, 1½ teaspoons pepper and ½ teaspoon paprika; set aside.

2. Season potatoes with remaining 1½ teaspoons garlic powder, 1½ teaspoons salt, 1½ teaspoons pepper and ½ teaspoon paprika. Add potatoes and onions to **CROCK-POT**® slow cooker. Cook on HIGH, stirring occasionally, until browned.

3. Return brisket to **CROCK-POT**® slow cooker. Add carrots and broth. Cover; cook on HIGH 4 to 5 hours or on LOW 8 to 10 hours, or until beef is tender.

Makes 6 to 8 servings

Beef with Apples and Sweet Potatoes

1 boneless beef chuck shoulder roast (about 2 pounds)	1 teaspoon salt
1 can (40 ounces) sweet potatoes, drained	1 teaspoon dried thyme, divided
2 small onions, sliced	¾ teaspoon black pepper, divided
2 apples, cored and sliced	1 tablespoon cornstarch
½ cup beef broth	¼ teaspoon ground cinnamon
2 cloves garlic, minced	2 tablespoons cold water

1. Trim excess fat from beef and discard. Cut beef into 2-inch pieces. Place beef, sweet potatoes, onions, apples, broth, garlic, salt, ½ teaspoon thyme and ½ teaspoon pepper in **CROCK-POT®** slow cooker. Cover; cook on LOW 8 to 9 hours.

2. Transfer beef, sweet potatoes and apples to platter; cover with foil to keep warm. Let cooking liquid stand 5 minutes to allow fat to rise. Skim off fat and discard.

3. Stir together cornstarch, remaining ½ teaspoon thyme, remaining ¼ teaspoon pepper, cinnamon and water until smooth; stir into cooking liquid. Cook 15 minutes on HIGH or until cooking liquid is thickened. Serve sauce over beef, sweet potatoes and apples.

Makes 6 servings

*Tip: Because **CROCK-POT®** slow cookers cook at a low heat for a long time, they're perfect for dishes calling for less-tender cuts of meat.*

Hot Beef Sandwiches au Jus

4 pounds beef rump roast

2 envelopes (1 ounce each) dried onion-flavor soup mix

2 teaspoons sugar

1 teaspoon dried oregano

1 tablespoon minced garlic

2 cans (10½ ounces each) beef broth

1 bottle (12 ounces) beer
Crusty French rolls, sliced in half

1. Trim excess fat from beef and discard. Place beef in **CROCK-POT®** slow cooker.

2. Combine soup mix, sugar, oregano, garlic, broth and beer in large mixing bowl. Pour mixture over beef. Cover; cook on HIGH 6 to 8 hours or until beef is fork-tender.

3. Remove beef from **CROCK-POT®** slow cooker. Shred beef with two forks. Return beef to cooking liquid; mix well. Serve on crusty rolls with extra cooking liquid ("jus") on side for dipping.

Makes 8 to 10 servings

Slow Cooker Stuffed Peppers

1 package (about 7 ounces) Spanish rice mix

1 pound lean ground beef

½ cup diced celery

1 small onion, chopped

1 egg, beaten

4 medium green bell peppers, halved lengthwise, cored and seeded

1 can (28 ounces) whole peeled tomatoes, undrained

1 can (10¾ ounces) condensed tomato soup, undiluted

1 cup water

1. Set aside seasoning packet from rice. Combine rice mix, beef, celery, onion and egg in large bowl. Divide meat mixture evenly among bell pepper halves.

2. Pour tomatoes with juice into **CROCK-POT®** slow cooker. Arrange filled bell pepper halves on top of tomatoes.

3. Combine tomato soup, water and reserved rice-mix seasoning packet in medium bowl. Pour over bell peppers. Cover; cook on LOW 8 to 10 hours.

Makes 4 servings

*Tip: Keep the lid on! The **CROCK-POT®** slow cooker can take as long as 30 minutes to regain the heat lost when the cover is removed. Only remove the cover when you're instructed to do so by the recipe.*

Osso Bucco

- 1 large onion, cut into thin wedges
- 2 large carrots, sliced
- 4 cloves garlic, sliced
- 4 meaty veal shanks (3 to 4 pounds)
- 2 teaspoons herbes de Provence or ½ teaspoon each dried thyme, rosemary, oregano and basil
- 1 teaspoon salt
- ½ teaspoon black pepper
- ¾ cup canned beef consommé or beef broth
- ¼ cup dry vermouth (optional)
- 3 tablespoons all-purpose flour
- 3 tablespoons water
- ¼ cup minced parsley
- 1 small clove garlic, minced
- 1 teaspoon grated lemon peel

1. Coat **CROCK-POT**® slow cooker with nonstick cooking spray. Place onion, carrots and sliced garlic in bottom. Arrange veal shanks over vegetables, overlapping slightly, and sprinkle herbes, salt and pepper over all. Add consommé and vermouth, if desired. Cover; cook on LOW 8 to 9 hours or on HIGH 5 to 6 hours or until shanks and vegetables are tender.

2. Transfer shanks and vegetables to serving platter; cover with foil to keep warm. Turn **CROCK-POT**® slow cooker to HIGH. Combine flour with 3 tablespoons water, mixing until smooth. Stir into cooking liquid. Cover; cook on HIGH 15 minutes or until sauce thickens.

3. Serve sauce over shanks and vegetables. Combine parsley, minced garlic and lemon peel; sprinkle over shanks and vegetables.

Makes 4 servings

Portuguese Madeira Beef Shanks

4 cloves garlic, minced

1 large white onion, diced

1 green bell pepper, cored and diced

2 jalapeño peppers, seeded and minced*

½ cup diced celery

½ cup minced parsley

4 medium beef shanks, bone in (about 3 pounds total)

1 tablespoon fresh rosemary, minced

1 teaspoon salt, or to taste

1 cup beef broth

1 cup dry Madeira wine

4 cups hot steamed rice

Horseradish sauce (optional)

*Jalapeño peppers can sting and irritate the skin, so wear rubber gloves when handling peppers and do not touch eyes.

1. Place garlic, onion, bell pepper, jalapeño peppers, celery and parsley in **CROCK-POT**® slow cooker.

2. Rub beef shanks with rosemary and salt. Place shanks on top of vegetables. Pour broth and wine over shanks and vegetables. Cover; cook on LOW 7 to 9 hours.

3. To serve, spoon 1 cup rice into each soup plate. Top rice with beef shank. Spoon vegetable sauce over shanks. Serve with horseradish sauce, if desired.

Makes 4 servings

Spanish-Style Couscous

1 pound lean ground beef

1 can (about 14 ounces) beef broth

1 small green bell pepper, cut into ½-inch pieces

½ cup pimiento-stuffed green olives, sliced

½ medium onion, chopped

2 cloves garlic, minced

1 teaspoon ground cumin

½ teaspoon dried thyme

1⅓ cups water

1 cup uncooked couscous

1. Brown beef in large skillet over medium-high heat, stirring to break up meat. Drain fat and discard.

2. Place broth, bell pepper, olives, onion, garlic, cumin, thyme and beef in **CROCK-POT®** slow cooker. Cover; cook on LOW 4 hours or until bell pepper is tender.

3. Bring water to a boil over high heat in small saucepan. Stir in couscous. Cover; remove from heat. Let stand 5 minutes; fluff with fork. Spoon couscous onto plates; top with beef mixture.

Makes 4 servings

Beefy Tostada Pie

2 teaspoons olive oil	1 can (15 ounces) tomato sauce
1½ cups chopped onion	1 cup sliced black olives
2 pounds ground beef	8 flour tortillas
1 teaspoon chili powder	4 cups shredded Cheddar cheese
1 teaspoon ground cumin	Sour cream, salsa and chopped green onion (optional)
1 teaspoon salt	
2 cloves garlic, minced	

1. Heat oil in large skillet over medium heat until hot. Add onion and cook until tender. Add ground beef, chili powder, cumin, salt and garlic; cook until browned. Stir in tomato sauce; heat through. Stir in black olives.

2. Make foil handles using three 18 × 2-inch strips of heavy foil, or use regular foil folded to double thickness. Place in **CROCK-POT**® slow cooker; crisscross foil to form spoke design. Lay one tortilla on foil strips. Spread with meat sauce and layer of cheese. Top with another tortilla, meat sauce and cheese. Repeat layers, ending with cheese. Cover and cook on HIGH 1½ hours.

3. To serve, lift out of **CROCK-POT**® slow cooker using foil handles and transfer to serving platter. Discard foil. Cut into wedges. Serve with sour cream, salsa and chopped green onion, if desired.

Makes 4 to 6 servings

Classic Beef and Noodles

1 tablespoon vegetable oil

2 pounds beef for stew, cut into 1-inch pieces

¼ pound fresh mushrooms, sliced into halves

2 tablespoons chopped onion

2 cloves garlic, minced

1 teaspoon salt

1 teaspoon dried oregano

½ teaspoon black pepper

¼ teaspoon dried marjoram

1 bay leaf

1½ cups beef broth

⅓ cup dry sherry

1 container (8 ounces) sour cream

½ cup all-purpose flour

¼ cup water

4 cups hot cooked noodles

1. Heat oil in large skillet over medium heat until hot. Brown beef on all sides. (Work in batches, if necessary.) Drain fat and discard.

2. Combine beef, mushrooms, onion, garlic, salt, oregano, pepper, marjoram and bay leaf in **CROCK-POT**® slow cooker. Pour in broth and sherry. Cover; cook on LOW 8 to 10 hours or on HIGH 4 to 5 hours. Remove bay leaf and discard.

3. Combine sour cream, flour and water in small bowl. Stir about 1 cup cooking liquid from **CROCK-POT**® slow cooker into sour cream mixture. Add mixture to **CROCK-POT**® slow cooker; mix well. Cook, uncovered, on HIGH 30 minutes or until thickened and bubbly. Serve over noodles.

Makes 8 servings

Sloppy Sloppy Joes

4 pounds ground beef

1 cup chopped onion

1 cup chopped green bell pepper

1 can (about 28 ounces) tomato sauce

2 cans (10¾ ounces each) condensed tomato soup, undiluted

1 cup packed brown sugar

¼ cup ketchup

3 tablespoons Worcestershire sauce

1 tablespoon dry mustard

1 tablespoon prepared mustard

1½ teaspoons chili powder

1 teaspoon garlic powder

Toasted hamburger buns

1. Brown beef in large skillet over medium-high heat, stirring to break up meat. Drain fat and discard.

2. Add onion and bell pepper; cook 5 to 10 minutes, stirring frequently, or until onion is translucent and mixture is fragrant.

3. Transfer meat mixture to **CROCK-POT®** slow cooker. Add remaining ingredients, except buns; stir until well blended. Cover; cook on LOW 4 to 6 hours. Serve on buns.

Makes 20 to 25 servings

Classic Spaghetti

- 2 tablespoons olive oil
- 2 onions, chopped
- 2 green bell peppers, sliced
- 2 stalks celery, sliced
- 4 teaspoons minced garlic
- 3 pounds lean ground beef
- 2 carrots, diced
- 1 cup sliced mushrooms
- 1 can (28 ounces) tomato sauce

- 1 can (28 ounces) stewed tomatoes, undrained
- 3 cups water
- 2 tablespoons minced parsley
- 1 tablespoon dried oregano
- 1 tablespoon sugar
- 2 teaspoons salt
- 2 teaspoons black pepper
- 1 pound uncooked spaghetti

1. Heat oil in large skillet over medium-high heat until hot. Add onion, bell peppers, celery and garlic; cook and stir until tender. Transfer to **CROCK-POT®** slow cooker.

2. In same skillet, brown ground beef. Drain and discard fat. Add beef, carrots, mushrooms, tomato sauce, tomatoes with juice, water, parsley, oregano, sugar, salt and black pepper to **CROCK-POT®** slow cooker. Cover; cook on LOW 6 to 8 hours or on HIGH 3 to 5 hours or until done.

3. Cook spaghetti according to package directions; drain. Serve sauce over cooked spaghetti.

Makes 6 to 8 servings

Barbecued Pulled Pork Sandwiches

- 1 (2½ pounds) pork shoulder roast
- 1 bottle (14 ounces) barbecue sauce
- 1 tablespoon fresh lemon juice
- 1 teaspoon brown sugar
- 1 medium onion, chopped
- 8 hamburger buns or hard rolls

1. Place pork roast in **CROCK-POT®** slow cooker. Cover; cook on LOW 10 to 12 hours or on HIGH 5 to 6 hours.

2. Remove pork roast from **CROCK-POT®** slow cooker. Shred with two forks. Discard cooking liquid. Return pork to **CROCK-POT®** slow cooker; add barbecue sauce, lemon juice, brown sugar and onion. Cover and cook on LOW 2 hours or on HIGH 1 hour. Serve on hamburger buns or hard rolls.

Makes 8 servings

Note: This kid-popular dish is sweet and savory, and most importantly, extremely easy to make. Serve with crunchy coleslaw on the side.

*Tip: For a 5-, 6- or 7-quart **CROCK-POT®** slow cooker, double all ingredients, except for the barbecue sauce. Increase the barbecue sauce to 21 ounces.*

Lemon Pork Chops

1 tablespoon vegetable oil

4 boneless pork chops

3 cans (8 ounces each) tomato sauce

1 large onion, quartered and sliced (optional)

1 large green bell pepper, cut into strips

1 tablespoon lemon-pepper seasoning

1 tablespoon Worcestershire sauce

1 large lemon, quartered
Lemon wedges (optional)

1. Heat oil in large skillet over medium-low heat until hot. Brown pork chops on both sides. Drain excess fat and discard. Transfer to **CROCK-POT**® slow cooker.

2. Combine tomato sauce, onion, if desired, bell pepper, lemon-pepper seasoning and Worcestershire sauce. Add to **CROCK-POT**® slow cooker.

3. Squeeze juice from lemon quarters over mixture; drop squeezed lemons into **CROCK-POT**® slow cooker. Cover; cook on LOW 6 to 8 hours or until pork is tender. Remove squeezed lemons before serving. Garnish with additional lemon wedges, if desired.

Makes 4 servings

*Tip: Browning pork before adding it to the **CROCK-POT**® slow cooker helps reduce the fat. Just remember to drain off the fat in the skillet before transferring the pork to the **CROCK-POT**® slow cooker.*

Scalloped Potatoes and Ham

6 **large russet potatoes, sliced into ¼-inch rounds**

1 **ham steak (about 1½ pounds), cut into cubes**

1 **can (10¾ ounces) condensed cream of mushroom soup, undiluted**

1 **soup can water**

4 **ounces shredded Cheddar cheese**

Grill seasoning, to taste

1. Grease inside of **CROCK-POT®** slow cooker with nonstick cooking spray. Layer potatoes and ham in prepared stoneware.

2. In a large mixing bowl, combine soup, water, cheese and seasoning; pour over potatoes and ham. Cover; cook on HIGH about 3½ hours or until potatoes are fork-tender. Turn to LOW and continue cooking about 1 hour more.

Makes 5 to 6 servings

Italian Sausage and Peppers

3 cups bell pepper chunks (1 inch), preferably a mix of red, yellow and green

1 small onion, cut into thin wedges

3 cloves garlic, minced

4 links hot or mild Italian sausage (about 1 pound)

1 cup marinara or pasta sauce

¼ cup red wine or port

1 tablespoon cornstarch

1 tablespoon water
   Hot cooked spaghetti

¼ cup grated Parmesan or Romano cheese

1. Coat **CROCK-POT**® slow cooker with nonstick cooking spray. Add bell peppers, onion and garlic. Arrange sausage over vegetables.

2. Combine pasta sauce and wine; pour over sausage. Cover; cook on LOW 8 to 9 hours or on HIGH 4 to 5 hours, or until sausage is cooked through and vegetables are very tender.

3. Transfer sausage to serving platter; cover with foil to keep warm. Skim off and discard fat from cooking liquid.

4. Turn heat to HIGH. Mix cornstarch with water until smooth; add to **CROCK-POT**® slow cooker. Cook 15 minutes or until sauce has thickened, stirring once. Serve sauce over spaghetti and sausage; top with cheese.

Makes 4 servings

Tip: Look for mixed bell pepper chunks at supermarket salad bars.

Pork and Tomato Ragoût

2 pounds pork stew meat, cut into 1-inch pieces

¼ cup all-purpose flour

3 tablespoons vegetable oil

1¼ cups white wine

2 pounds red potatoes, cut into ½-inch pieces

1 can (14½ ounces) diced tomatoes, undrained

1 cup finely chopped onion

1 cup water

½ cup finely chopped celery

2 cloves garlic, minced

½ teaspoon black pepper

1 cinnamon stick

3 tablespoons chopped fresh parsley

1. Toss pork with flour. Heat oil in large skillet over medium-high heat until hot. Add pork to skillet and brown on all sides. Transfer to **CROCK-POT®** slow cooker.

2. Add wine to skillet; bring to a boil, scraping up browned bits from bottom of skillet. Pour into **CROCK-POT®** slow cooker.

3. Add all remaining ingredients except parsley. Cover; cook on LOW 6 to 8 hours or until pork and potatoes are tender. Remove and discard cinnamon stick. Adjust seasonings, if desired. To serve, sprinkle with parsley.

Makes 6 servings

*Tip: Vegetables such as potatoes and carrots can sometimes take longer to cook in a **CROCK-POT®** slow cooker than meat. Place evenly cut vegetables along the sides of the **CROCK-POT®** slow cooker when possible.*

Pork Loin with Sherry and Red Onions

- 3 large red onions, thinly sliced
- 1 cup pearl onions, blanched and peeled
- 2 tablespoons unsalted butter or margarine
- 2½ pounds boneless pork loin, tied
- ½ teaspoon salt
- ½ teaspoon freshly ground black pepper
- ½ cup cooking sherry
- 2 tablespoons fresh chopped Italian parsley
- 1½ tablespoons cornstarch
- 2 tablespoons water

1. Cook red and pearl onions in butter in medium skillet over medium heat until soft.

2. Rub pork loin with salt and pepper and place in **CROCK-POT®** slow cooker. Add cooked onions, sherry and parsley. Cover; cook on LOW 8 to 10 hours or on HIGH 5 to 6 hours.

3. Remove pork loin; cover and let stand 15 minutes before slicing.

4. Turn heat to HIGH. Combine cornstarch and water and stir into cooking liquid in **CROCK-POT®** slow cooker. Cook 15 minutes or until sauce has thickened. Serve sliced pork loin with onions and sherry sauce.

Makes 8 servings

Tip: If using the 5-, 6- or 7-quart **CROCK-POT®** *slow cooker, double all ingredients, except for the sherry, cornstarch and water.*

Slow Cooker Cassoulet

1 pound white beans, such as Great Northern

Boiling water to cover beans

1 tablespoon butter

1 tablespoon canola oil

4 veal shanks, 1½ inches thick, tied for cooking

3 cups beef broth

4 ounces maple-smoked bacon or pancetta, diced

3 cloves garlic, smashed

1 sprig each thyme and savory or 1 tablespoon each dried thyme and dried savory

2 whole cloves

Salt and black pepper, to taste

4 mild Italian sausages

1. Rinse and sort beans and place in large bowl; cover completely with water. Soak 6 to 8 hours or overnight. (To quick-soak beans, place beans in large saucepan; cover with water. Bring to a boil over high heat. Boil 2 minutes. Remove from heat; let soak, covered, 1 hour.) Drain beans; discard water.

2. Heat butter and oil in large skillet over medium-high heat until hot. Sear shanks on all sides until browned. Transfer to **CROCK-POT**® slow cooker. Add broth, bacon, garlic, beans, herbs and cloves. Add enough water to cover beans, if needed. Cover; cook on LOW 8 hours. After 4 hours, check liquid and add boiling water as needed to barely cover beans.

3. Before serving, season with salt and pepper. Grill sausages; serve with cassoulet.

Makes 4 servings

Fall-off-the-Bone BBQ Ribs

½ **cup paprika**

⅜ **cup sugar**

¼ **cup onion powder**

1½ **teaspoons salt**

1½ **teaspoons black pepper**

2½ **pounds pork baby back ribs, silver skin removed**

1 **can (20 ounces) beer or beef stock**

1 **quart barbecue sauce**

½ **cup honey**

White sesame seeds and sliced chives (optional)

1. Preheat grill. Lightly oil grill grate.

2. While grill heats, combine paprika, sugar, onion powder, salt and pepper in large mixing bowl. Generously season ribs with dry rub mixture. Place ribs on grill. Cook for 3 minutes on each side or until ribs have grill marks.

3. Portion ribs into sections of 3 to 4 bones. Place in **CROCK-POT**® slow cooker. Pour beer over ribs. Cover; cook on HIGH 2 hours. Blend barbecue sauce and honey and add. Cover; cook 1½ hours longer. Garnish with white sesame seeds and chives, if desired. Serve with extra sauce on the side.

Makes 6 to 8 servings

Vegetable-Stuffed Pork Chops

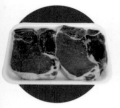   

4 **double pork rib chops, well trimmed**
Salt and black pepper, to taste
1 **can (15¼ ounces) kernel corn, drained**
1 **green bell pepper, chopped**

1 **cup Italian-style seasoned dry bread crumbs**
1 **small onion, chopped**
½ **cup uncooked converted long-grain rice**
1 **can (8 ounces) tomato sauce**

1. Cut pocket into each pork chop, cutting from edge nearest bone. Lightly season pockets with salt and pepper to taste. Combine corn, bell pepper, bread crumbs, onion and rice in large bowl. Stuff pork chops with rice mixture. Secure open side with toothpicks.

2. Place any remaining rice mixture in **CROCK-POT**® slow cooker. Add stuffed pork chops to **CROCK-POT**® slow cooker. Moisten top of each pork chop with tomato sauce. Pour in any remaining tomato sauce. Cover; cook on LOW 8 to 10 hours.

3. Transfer pork chops to serving platter. Remove and discard toothpicks. Serve with extra rice mixture.

Makes 4 servings

Tip: Your butcher can cut a pocket in the pork chops to save you time and to ensure even cooking.

Pork Chops with Jalapeño-Pecan Cornbread Stuffing

6 boneless (1½ pounds) loin pork chops, 1-inch thick

¾ cup chopped onion

¾ cup chopped celery

½ cup coarsely chopped pecans

½ medium jalapeño pepper, seeded and chopped*

1 teaspoon rubbed sage

½ teaspoon dried rosemary

⅛ teaspoon black pepper

4 cups unseasoned cornbread stuffing mix

1¼ cups reduced-sodium chicken broth

1 egg, lightly beaten

*Jalapeño peppers can sting and irritate the skin, so wear rubber gloves when handling peppers and do not touch eyes.

1. Trim excess fat from pork and discard. Coat large skillet with nonstick cooking spray; heat over medium heat until hot. Add pork; cook 10 minutes or until browned on both sides. Remove; set aside.

2. Add onion, celery, pecans, jalapeño pepper, sage, rosemary and black pepper to skillet. Cook 5 minutes or until onion and celery are tender.

3. Combine cornbread stuffing mix, vegetable mixture and broth in medium bowl. Stir in egg. Spoon stuffing mixture into **CROCK-POT®** slow cooker. Arrange pork on top. Cover; cook on LOW about 5 hours or until pork is tender.

Makes 6 servings

Note: *For a more moist dressing, increase chicken broth to 1½ cups.*

Sauerkraut Pork Ribs

1 tablespoon vegetable oil	¼ to ½ teaspoon black pepper
3 to 4 pounds pork country-style ribs	¾ cup water
1 large onion, thinly sliced	2 jars (about 28 ounces each) sauerkraut
1 teaspoon caraway seeds	12 medium red potatoes, quartered
½ teaspoon garlic powder	

1. Heat oil in large skillet over medium-low heat until hot. Brown ribs on all sides. Transfer to **CROCK-POT®** slow cooker. Drain excess fat and discard.

2. Add onion to skillet; cook until tender. Add caraway seeds, garlic powder and pepper; cook 15 minutes. Transfer onion mixture to **CROCK-POT®** slow cooker.

3. Add water to skillet and scrape up any brown bits. Pour pan juices into **CROCK-POT®** slow cooker. Partially drain sauerkraut, leaving some liquid; pour over meat. Top with potatoes. Cover; cook on LOW 6 to 8 hours or until potatoes are tender, stirring once during cooking.

Makes 12 servings

poultry

Mediterranean Chicken

- 1 **tablespoon olive oil**
- 2 **pounds boneless, skinless chicken breasts**
  Juice of 2 lemons
- 2 **cinnamon sticks**
- 6 **teaspoons minced garlic**
- 1 **can (28 ounces) diced tomatoes, undrained**

- 1 **bay leaf**
- ½ **teaspoon pepper**
- ½ **cup sherry**
- 2 **onions, chopped**
- 1 **pound cooked broad noodles**
- ½ **cup feta cheese**

1. Heat oil in large skillet. Add chicken and lightly brown.

2. Combine lemon juice, cinnamon, garlic, tomatoes with juice, bay leaf, pepper, sherry and onions in **CROCK-POT®** slow cooker. Add chicken. Cover; cook on LOW 8 to 10 hours or on HIGH 4 to 5 hours or until done.

3. Discard cinnamon sticks and bay leaf. Serve chicken and sauce over cooked noodles. Sprinkle with cheese just before serving.

Makes 6 servings

Chicken Provençal

2 pounds boneless, skinless chicken thighs, each cut into quarters

2 medium red peppers, cut into ¼-inch-thick slices

1 medium yellow pepper, cut into ¼-inch-thick slices

1 onion, thinly sliced

1 can (28 ounces) plum tomatoes, drained

3 cloves garlic, minced

¼ teaspoon salt

¼ teaspoon thyme

¼ teaspoon fennel seeds, crushed

3 strips orange peel

½ cup fresh basil leaves, chopped

1. Place thighs, bell peppers, onion, tomatoes, garlic, salt, thyme, fennel seeds and orange peel in **CROCK-POT**® slow cooker. Mix thoroughly.

2. Cover; cook on LOW 7 to 9 hours or on HIGH 3 to 4 hours. Sprinkle with basil to serve.

Makes 8 servings

Note: *This Southern French chicken dish contrasts the citrus with the sweet. Serve with a crusty French baguette and seasonal vegetables.*

Tip: *Recipe can be doubled for a 5-, 6- or 7-quart* **CROCK-POT**® *slow cooker.*

Fresh Herbed Turkey Breast

2 tablespoons butter, softened

¼ cup fresh sage leaves, minced

¼ cup fresh tarragon leaves, minced

1 clove garlic, minced

1 teaspoon black pepper

½ teaspoon salt

1 (4-pound) split turkey breast

1½ tablespoons cornstarch

1. Mix together butter, sage, tarragon, garlic, pepper and salt. Rub butter mixture all over turkey breast.

2. Place turkey breast in **CROCK-POT**® slow cooker. Cover; cook on LOW 8 to 10 hours or on HIGH 4 to 5 hours or until turkey is no longer pink in center.

3. Remove turkey breast from **CROCK-POT**® slow cooker. Turn heat to HIGH; slowly whisk in cornstarch to thicken juices. When sauce is thick and smooth, pour over turkey breast. Slice to serve.

Makes 8 servings

Note: Fresh herbs enliven this simple, excellent main dish.

Tip: Recipe can be doubled for a 5-, 6- or 7-quart CROCK-POT® slow cooker.

Turkey Tacos

1 **pound lean ground turkey**	1 **tablespoon butter**
1 **medium onion, chopped**	1 **tablespoon all-purpose flour**
1 **can (6 ounces) tomato paste**	¼ **teaspoon salt**
½ **cup chunky salsa**	⅓ **cup milk**
1 **tablespoon chopped fresh cilantro**	½ **cup sour cream**
½ **teaspoon salt**	**Ground red pepper, to taste**
	8 **taco shells**

1. Brown turkey and onion in large skillet over medium heat, stirring to break up meat. Combine turkey mixture, tomato paste, salsa, cilantro and salt in **CROCK-POT®** slow cooker. Cover; cook on LOW 4 to 5 hours.

2. Just before serving, melt butter in small saucepan over low heat. Stir in flour and salt; cook 1 minute. Carefully stir in milk. Cook and stir over low heat until thickened. Remove from heat. Combine sour cream and sprinkle of ground red pepper in small bowl. Stir into hot milk mixture. Return to heat; cook over low heat 1 minute, stirring constantly.

3. To serve, spoon ¼ cup turkey mixture into each taco shell. Spoon sour cream mixture over taco filling.

Makes 8 servings

*Tip: When adapting conventionally prepared recipes for your **CROCK-POT®** slow cooker, revise the amount of herbs and spices you use. For example, whole herbs and spices increase in flavor while ground spices tend to lose flavor during slow cooking. If you prefer, you can adjust the seasonings or add herbs and spices just before serving the dish.*

Chicken Sausage
with Peppers and Basil

1   tablespoon olive oil

1   clove garlic, minced

½   yellow onion, minced (about ½ cup)

1   pound sweet or hot Italian chicken sausage

1   can (28 ounces) whole tomatoes, drained and seeded

½   red bell pepper, cut into ½-inch slices

½   yellow bell pepper, cut into ½-inch slices

½   orange bell pepper, cut into ½-inch slices

¾   cup chopped fresh basil
    Crushed red pepper flakes, to taste
    Salt and black pepper, to taste
    Hot cooked pasta

1. Heat oil in large skillet over medium heat until hot. Add garlic and onion, and cook until translucent.

2. Remove sausage from casing and cut into 1-inch chunks. Add to skillet and cook 3 to 4 minutes or until just beginning to brown. Transfer to **CROCK-POT®** slow cooker with slotted spoon, skimming off some fat.

3. Add tomatoes, bell peppers, basil, pepper flakes, salt and black pepper to **CROCK-POT®** slow cooker and stir to blend. Cook on HIGH 2½ to 3 hours or until peppers have softened. Adjust seasonings to taste. Serve over pasta.

Makes 4 servings

Autumn Chicken

1 **can (14 ounces) whole artichoke hearts, drained**

1 **can (14 ounces) whole mushrooms, divided**

12 **boneless, skinless chicken breasts**

1 **jar (6½ ounces) marinated artichoke hearts, with liquid**

¾ **cup white wine**

½ **cup balsamic vinaigrette**

Hot cooked noodles

Paprika for garnish (optional)

Spread whole artichokes over bottom of **CROCK-POT®** slow cooker. Top with half of mushrooms. Layer chicken over mushrooms. Add marinated artichoke hearts with liquid. Add remaining mushrooms. Pour in wine and vinaigrette. Cover; cook on LOW 4 to 5 hours. Serve over noodles. Garnish with paprika, if desired.

Makes 10 to 12 servings

Tarragon Turkey and Pasta

1½ to 2 pounds turkey tenderloins

½ cup thinly sliced celery

¼ cup thinly sliced green onions

4 tablespoons fresh tarragon, minced

¼ cup dry white wine

1 teaspoon salt

1 teaspoon freshly ground black pepper

½ cup plain yogurt

1 tablespoon fresh minced Italian parsley

1 tablespoon lemon juice

1½ tablespoons cornstarch

2 tablespoons water

4 cups pasta of your choice, cooked al denté

1. Combine turkey, celery, green onions, 2 tablespoons fresh tarragon, wine, salt and pepper in **CROCK-POT®** slow cooker. Mix thoroughly. Cover; cook on LOW 6 to 8 hours or on HIGH 3½ to 4 hours or until turkey is no longer pink.

2. Remove turkey; cut into ½-inch-thick medallions. Turn **CROCK-POT®** slow cooker to HIGH. Stir yogurt, remaining 2 tablespoons fresh tarragon, parsley and lemon juice into cooking liquid.

3. Combine cornstarch and water in small bowl. Stir into cooking liquid and cook until thickened. Serve turkey medallions over pasta. Drizzle with tarragon sauce.

Makes 4 servings

Note: *This easy dish is elegant enough to serve at a dinner party.*

Tip: *Recipe can be doubled for a 5-, 6- or 7-quart* **CROCK-POT®** *slow cooker.*

Thai Chicken

2½ **pounds chicken pieces**

1 **cup hot salsa**

¼ **cup peanut butter**

2 **tablespoons lime juice**

1 **tablespoon soy sauce**

1 **teaspoon minced fresh ginger**

½ **cup peanuts, chopped**

2 **tablespoons chopped fresh cilantro**

Hot cooked rice (optional)

1. Place chicken in **CROCK-POT**® slow cooker. Mix together salsa, peanut butter, lime juice, soy sauce and ginger; pour over chicken.

2. Cover; cook on LOW 8 to 9 hours or on HIGH 3 to 4 hours or until done.

3. Serve over rice, if desired, topped with sauce, peanuts and cilantro.

Makes 6 servings

Mu Shu Turkey

1 can (16 ounces) plums, drained and pitted

½ cup orange juice

¼ cup finely chopped onion

1 tablespoon minced fresh ginger

¼ teaspoon ground cinnamon

1 pound boneless, skinless turkey breast, cut into thin strips

6 (7-inch) flour tortillas

3 cups coleslaw mix

1. Place plums in blender or food processor. Cover; blend until almost smooth. Combine plums, orange juice, onion, ginger and cinnamon in **CROCK-POT**® slow cooker; mix well.

2. Place turkey over plum mixture. Cover; cook on LOW 3 to 4 hours.

3. Remove turkey from **CROCK-POT**® slow cooker. Divide evenly among tortillas. Spoon about 2 tablespoons plum sauce over turkey in each tortilla; top with about ½ cup coleslaw mix. Fold up bottom edge of tortilla over filling, fold in sides and roll up to enclose filling. Repeat with remaining tortillas. Use remaining plum sauce for dipping.

Makes 6 servings

Tip: To slightly thicken a sauce in the CROCK-POT® slow cooker, remove the solid foods and leave the sauce in the CROCK-POT® slow cooker. Mix 1 to 2 tablespoons cornstarch with ¼ cup cold water until smooth. Stir mixture into the sauce and cook on HIGH until the sauce is thickened.

Easy Parmesan Chicken

8 ounces mushrooms, sliced

1 medium onion, cut into thin wedges

1 tablespoon olive oil

4 boneless, skinless chicken breasts

1 jar (26 ounces) pasta sauce

½ teaspoon dried basil

¼ teaspoon dried oregano

1 bay leaf

½ cup (2 ounces) shredded part-skim mozzarella cheese

¼ cup grated Parmesan cheese

Hot cooked spaghetti

1. Place mushrooms and onion in **CROCK-POT®** slow cooker.

2. Heat oil in large skillet over medium-high heat until hot. Lightly brown chicken on both sides. Place chicken in **CROCK-POT®** slow cooker. Pour pasta sauce over chicken; add basil, oregano and bay leaf. Cover; cook on LOW 6 to 7 hours or on HIGH 3 to 4 hours, or until chicken is tender. Remove and discard bay leaf.

3. Sprinkle chicken with cheeses. Cook, uncovered, on LOW 15 to 30 minutes or until cheeses have melted. Serve over spaghetti.

Makes 4 servings

*Tip: Dairy products should be added at the end of the cooking time because they will curdle if cooked in the **CROCK-POT®** slow cooker for a long time.*

Moroccan Chicken Tagine

3 pounds bone-in chicken pieces, skin removed

2 cups chicken broth

1 can (14½ ounces) diced tomatoes, undrained

2 onions, chopped

1 cup chopped dried apricots

4 cloves garlic, minced

2 teaspoons ground cumin

1 teaspoon ground ginger

1 teaspoon ground cinnamon

½ teaspoon ground coriander

½ teaspoon ground red pepper

6 sprigs fresh cilantro

1 tablespoon cornstarch

1 tablespoon water

1 can (15 ounces) chickpeas, drained and rinsed

2 tablespoons chopped fresh cilantro

¼ cup slivered almonds, toasted

Hot cooked rice or couscous

1. Place chicken in **CROCK-POT®** slow cooker. Combine broth, tomatoes with juice, onions, apricots, garlic, cumin, ginger, cinnamon, coriander, red pepper and cilantro in medium bowl; pour over chicken. Cover; cook on LOW 4 to 5 hours or until chicken is cooked through.

2. Transfer chicken to serving platter; cover with foil to keep warm. Combine cornstarch and water in small bowl, stirring until smooth. Stir cornstarch mixture and chickpeas into **CROCK-POT®** slow cooker. Cover; cook on HIGH 15 minutes or until sauce has thickened.

3. Pour sauce over chicken. Sprinkle with cilantro and toasted almonds, and serve over rice.

Makes 4 to 6 servings

Tip: To toast almonds, heat small nonstick skillet over medium-high heat. Add almonds; cook and stir about 3 minutes or until golden brown. Remove from pan immediately. Cool before adding to other ingredients.

Simple Coq au Vin

4 chicken legs
  Salt and black pepper, to taste
2 tablespoons olive oil
8 ounces fresh mushrooms, sliced
1 onion, sliced into rings

½ cup red wine
½ teaspoon dried basil
½ teaspoon dried thyme
½ teaspoon dried oregano
  Hot cooked rice

1. Sprinkle chicken with salt and pepper. Heat oil in large skillet over medium-high heat until hot. Brown chicken on both sides. Transfer chicken to **CROCK-POT®** slow cooker.

2. Add mushrooms and onion to skillet; cook and stir until onions are tender. Add wine; stir and scrape brown bits from bottom of skillet. Add mixture to **CROCK-POT®** slow cooker. Sprinkle with basil, thyme and oregano. Cover; cook on LOW 8 to 10 hours or on HIGH 3 to 4 hours.

3. Serve chicken and sauce over rice.

Makes 4 servings

Mexican Chili Chicken

2 medium green bell peppers, cut into thin strips

1 large onion, quartered and thinly sliced

4 chicken thighs

4 chicken drumsticks

1 tablespoon chili powder

2 teaspoons dried oregano

1 jar (16 ounces) chipotle salsa

½ cup ketchup

2 teaspoons ground cumin

½ teaspoon salt

Hot cooked noodles

1. Place bell peppers and onion in **CROCK-POT®** slow cooker; top with chicken. Sprinkle chili powder and oregano evenly over chicken. Add salsa. Cover; cook on LOW 7 to 8 hours or on HIGH 2 to 3 hours or until chicken is tender.

2. Transfer chicken to serving bowl; cover with foil to keep warm. Stir ketchup, cumin and salt into cooking liquid. Cook, uncovered, on HIGH 15 minutes or until hot.

3. Pour mixture over chicken. Serve chicken and sauce over noodles.

Makes 4 servings

Tip: For thicker sauce, blend 1 tablespoon cornstarch and 2 tablespoons water. Stir into cooking liquid with ketchup, cumin and salt.

New England Clam Chowder

6 slices bacon, diced

2 onions, chopped

5 cans (6½ ounces each) clams, drained and liquid reserved

6 medium red potatoes, cubed

2 tablespoons minced garlic

1 teaspoon black pepper

2 cans (12 ounces each) evaporated milk

Salt, to taste

1. Cook and stir bacon and onion in medium skillet until onions are tender. Place in **CROCK-POT®** slow cooker.

2. Add enough water to reserved clam liquid to make 3 cups. Pour into **CROCK-POT®** slow cooker, and add potatoes, garlic and pepper. Cover; cook on LOW 5 to 8 hours or HIGH 1 to 3 hours.

3. Turn **CROCK-POT®** slow cooker to LOW and mix in reserved clams and milk. Cover; cook 30 to 45 minutes. Adjust seasoning, if necessary.

Makes 6 to 8 servings

*Tip: Seafood is delicate and should be added to the **CROCK-POT®** slow cooker during the last 15 to 30 minutes of the cooking time if you're using the HIGH heat setting, and during the last 30 to 45 minutes if you're using the LOW setting. Seafood overcooks easily, becoming tough and rubbery, so watch your cooking times, and cook only long enough for seafood to be done.*

Creamy Slow Cooker Seafood Chowder

- 1 quart (4 cups) half-and-half
- 2 cans (14½ ounces each) whole white potatoes, drained and cubed
- 2 cans (10¾ ounces) condensed cream of mushroom soup, undiluted
- 1 bag (16 ounces) frozen hash brown potatoes
- 1 medium onion, minced
- ½ cup (1 stick) butter, cubed
- 1 teaspoon salt
- 1 teaspoon black pepper
- 5 cans (about 8 ounces each) whole oysters, drained and rinsed
- 2 cans (about 6 ounces each) minced clams
- 2 cans (about 4 ounces each) cocktail shrimp, drained and rinsed

1. Combine half-and-half, canned potatoes, soup, frozen potatoes, onion, butter, salt and pepper in **CROCK-POT®** slow cooker. Mix well. Cover; cook on LOW 3½ to 4½ hours.

2. Add oysters, clams and shrimp; stir gently. Cover; cook on LOW 30 to 45 minutes, or until done.

Makes 8 to 10 servings

Sweet and Sour Shrimp with Pineapple

   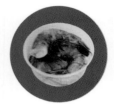

3 cans (8 ounces each) pineapple chunks, drained and 1 cup juice reserved

2 packages (6 ounces each) frozen snow peas, thawed

¼ cup cornstarch

⅓ cup sugar, plus 2 teaspoons

2 chicken bouillon cubes

2 cups boiling water

4 teaspoons soy sauce

1 teaspoon ground ginger

1 pound shrimp, peeled, deveined and cleaned*

¼ cup cider vinegar

Hot cooked rice

*or 1 pound frozen, peeled, deveined shrimp, unthawed

1. Drain pineapple chunks, reserving 1 cup juice. Place pineapple and snow peas in **CROCK-POT®** slow cooker.

2. Combine cornstarch and sugar in medium saucepan. Dissolve bouillon cubes in water and add to saucepan. Mix in 1 cup reserved pineapple juice, soy sauce and ginger. Bring to a boil and cook for 1 minute. Pour into **CROCK-POT®** slow cooker. Cover; cook on LOW 4½ to 5½ hours.

3. Add shrimp and vinegar. Cover; cook on LOW 30 minutes or until shrimp are done. Serve over hot rice.

Makes 4 servings

Manhattan Clam Chowder

3 slices bacon, diced

2 stalks celery, chopped

3 onions, chopped

2 cups water

1 can (15 ounces) stewed tomatoes, undrained and chopped

4 small red potatoes, diced

2 carrots, diced

½ teaspoon dried thyme

½ teaspoon black pepper

½ teaspoon Louisiana-style hot sauce

1 pound minced clams*

*If fresh clams are unavailable, use canned clams; 6 (6½-ounce) cans yield about 1 pound of clam meat; drain and discard liquid.

1. Cook and stir bacon in medium saucepan until bacon is crisp. Remove bacon and place in **CROCK-POT®** slow cooker.

2. Add celery and onions to skillet. Cook and stir until tender. Place in **CROCK-POT®** slow cooker.

3. Mix in water, tomatoes with juice, potatoes, carrots, thyme, pepper and hot sauce. Cover; cook on LOW 6 to 8 hours or HIGH 4 to 6 hours. Add clams during last half hour of cooking.

Makes 4 servings

Cream of Scallop Soup

1½ **pounds red potatoes, cubed**

3 **cups water**

1½ **cups milk**

2 **onions, chopped**

2 **carrots, shredded**

½ **cup vegetable broth**

2 **tablespoons white wine**

½ **teaspoon garlic powder**

½ **teaspoon dried thyme**

2 **egg yolks, lightly beaten**

1 **pound sea scallops**

1 **cup shredded Cheddar cheese**

1. Combine potatoes, water, milk, onions, carrots, broth, wine, garlic powder and thyme in **CROCK-POT**® slow cooker. Cover; cook on LOW 6 to 8 hours or HIGH 3 to 5 hours.

2. Turn **CROCK-POT**® slow cooker to LOW and mix in egg yolks. Cover; cook on LOW 1 hour.

3. Add scallops and cook, uncovered, on LOW 10 to 20 minutes. Before serving, mix in cheese and cook, uncovered, on LOW 5 minutes or until cheese has melted.

Makes 4 to 6 servings

Tip: Scallops cook very quickly; overcooking will make them tough, so check for doneness early. Small bay scallops will cook more quickly than larger sea scallops.

Shrimp Creole

   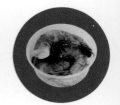

¼ cup (½ stick) butter

1 onion, chopped

¼ cup biscuit baking mix

3 cups water

1 cup chopped celery

1 cup chopped green bell pepper

2 cans (6 ounces each) tomato paste

2 teaspoons salt

½ teaspoon sugar

2 bay leaves

Black pepper, to taste

4 pounds shrimp, peeled, deveined and cleaned

Hot cooked rice

1. Cook and stir butter and onion in medium skillet over reduced heat until onion is tender. Stir in biscuit mix. Place mixture in **CROCK-POT®** slow cooker.

2. Add water, celery, bell pepper, tomato paste, salt, sugar, bay leaves and black pepper. Cover; cook on LOW 6 to 8 hours.

3. Turn **CROCK-POT®** slow cooker to HIGH and add shrimp. Cook on HIGH 45 minutes to 1 hour or until shrimp are done. Remove bay leaves. Serve over rice.

Makes 8 to 10 servings

Caribbean Shrimp with Rice

1 package (12 ounces) frozen shrimp, thawed

½ cup fat-free, reduced-sodium chicken broth

1 clove garlic, minced

1 teaspoon chili powder

½ teaspoon salt

½ teaspoon dried oregano

1 cup frozen peas, thawed

½ cup diced tomatoes

2 cups cooked long-grain white rice

1. Combine shrimp, broth, garlic, chili powder, salt and oregano in **CROCK-POT®** slow cooker. Cover; cook on LOW 2 hours.

2. Add peas and tomatoes. Cover; cook on LOW 5 minutes. Stir in rice. Cover; cook on LOW 5 minutes longer, or until rice is heated through.

Makes 4 servings

soups, stews & chilies

Mexican Cheese Soup

- 1 **pound processed cheese, cubed**
- 1 **pound ground beef, cooked and drained**
- 1 **can (8³/₄ ounces) whole kernel corn, undrained**
- 1 **can (15 ounces) kidney beans, undrained**
- 1 **jalapeño pepper, seeded and diced* (optional)**

- 1 **can (14¹/₂ ounces) diced tomatoes with green chilies, undrained**
- 1 **can (14¹/₂ ounces) stewed tomatoes, undrained**
- 1 **envelope taco seasoning**

*Jalapeño peppers can sting and irritate the skin; wear rubber gloves when handling peppers and do not touch eyes. Wash hands after handling.

1. Coat inside of **CROCK-POT**® slow cooker with nonstick cooking spray. Combine cheese, beef, corn, beans with liquid, jalapeño, if desired, tomatoes with chilies, stewed tomatoes and taco seasoning in prepared **CROCK-POT**® slow cooker.

2. Cover; cook on LOW 4 to 5 hours or on HIGH 3 hours or until done. Serve with corn chips, if desired.

Makes 6 to 8 servings

Mama's Beer Chili

2 tablespoons olive oil

1 large onion (Vidalia if available), diced

4 cloves garlic, crushed

1½ to 2 pounds ground turkey

1 can (28 ounces) crushed tomatoes

1 cup beer (dark preferred)

3 tablespoons chili powder

1 teaspoon curry powder

3 tablespoons hot pepper sauce

⅓ cup honey

1 package (10 ounces) frozen corn

1 can (15 ounces) pink or kidney beans, rinsed and drained

⅓ cup diced mild green chilies

3 beef bouillon cubes

1 to 2 tablespoons flour, to thicken

1. Heat oil in large skillet over medium-low heat until hot. Add onion. Cook and stir 5 minutes. Add garlic; cook and stir 2 minutes.

2. Add turkey to skillet. Cook and stir until turkey is no longer pink. Drain fat and discard.

3. Add remaining ingredients, stirring until mixed. Transfer to **CROCK-POT®** slow cooker. Cover; cook on LOW 8 to 10 hours or on HIGH 4 to 6 hours.

Makes 4 to 6 servings

Tip: Serve with cornbread and jam, or a loaf of fresh bread, if desired.

Beef Stew with Bacon, Onion and Sweet Potatoes

   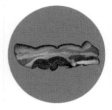

1 pound beef for stew, cut into 1-inch chunks

1 can (14½ ounces) beef broth

2 medium sweet potatoes, peeled and cut into 2-inch chunks

1 large onion, cut into 1½-inch chunks

2 slices thick-cut bacon, diced

1 teaspoon dried thyme

1 teaspoon salt

¼ teaspoon black pepper

2 tablespoons cornstarch

2 tablespoons water

1. Coat **CROCK-POT**® slow cooker with nonstick cooking spray. Combine all ingredients except cornstarch and water in **CROCK-POT**® slow cooker; mix well. Cover; cook on LOW 7 to 8 hours or on HIGH 4 to 5 hours, or until meat and vegetables are tender.

2. With slotted spoon, transfer beef and vegetables to serving bowl; cover with foil to keep warm.

3. Turn **CROCK-POT**® slow cooker to HIGH. Combine cornstarch and water; stir until smooth. Stir into cooking liquid. Cover; cook 15 minutes or until thickened. To serve, spoon sauce over beef and vegetables.

Makes 4 servings

Minestrone Alla Milanese

1 cup diced red potatoes

1 cup coarsely chopped carrots

2 cans (14½ ounces each) beef broth

1 can (14½ ounces) diced tomatoes, undrained

1 cup coarsely chopped green cabbage

1 cup sliced zucchini

¾ cup chopped onion

¾ cup sliced fresh green beans

¾ cup coarsely chopped celery

¾ cup water

2 tablespoons olive oil

1 clove garlic, minced

½ teaspoon dried basil

¼ teaspoon dried rosemary

1 bay leaf

1 can (15 ounces) cannellini beans, rinsed and drained

Shredded Parmesan cheese (optional)

1. Combine all ingredients except cannellini beans and cheese in **CROCK-POT®** slow cooker; mix well. Cover; cook on LOW 5 to 6 hours.

2. Add cannellini beans. Cover; cook on LOW 1 hour or until vegetables are tender.

3. Remove and discard bay leaf. Garnish with cheese, if desired.

Makes 8 to 10 servings

Bean and Corn Chili

2 medium onions, finely chopped

5 cloves garlic, minced

½ teaspoon olive oil

2 tablespoons red wine

1 green bell pepper, seeded and finely chopped

1 red bell pepper, seeded and finely chopped

1 stalk celery, finely sliced

6 Roma tomatoes, chopped

2 cans (15 ounces) kidney beans, rinsed and drained

1 can (6 ounces) tomato paste

1 cup frozen corn kernels

1 teaspoon salt

1 teaspoon chili powder

½ teaspoon black pepper

¼ teaspoon cumin

¼ teaspoon ground red pepper

¼ teaspoon dried oregano

¼ teaspoon ground coriander

1½ cups nonfat chicken or vegetable broth

1. Cook onions and garlic in olive oil and red wine in a medium skillet until onions are tender. Add onion mixture and bell peppers, celery, tomatoes, beans, tomato paste, corn, salt, chili powder, black pepper, cumin, ground red pepper, oregano, coriander and broth to **CROCK-POT®** slow cooker. Mix thoroughly.

2. Cover; cook on LOW 6 to 8 hours or on HIGH 3 to 4 hours.

Makes 6 servings

Note: *Hearty yet low in fat, this chili will warm you on any winter evening.*

Tip: *Recipe can be doubled for a 5-, 6- or 7-quart* **CROCK-POT®** *slow cooker.*

Chicken and Black Bean Chili

1 pound boneless, skinless chicken thighs, cut into 1-inch chunks

2 teaspoons chili powder

2 teaspoons ground cumin

¾ teaspoon salt

1 green bell pepper, diced

1 small onion, chopped

3 cloves garlic, minced

1 can (14½ ounces) diced tomatoes, undrained

1 cup chunky salsa

1 can (about 15 ounces) black beans, rinsed and drained

Toppings: sour cream, diced ripe avocado, shredded Cheddar cheese, sliced green onions or chopped cilantro, crushed tortilla or corn chips

1. Combine chicken, chili powder, cumin and salt in **CROCK-POT®** slow cooker, tossing to coat.

2. Add bell pepper, onion and garlic; mix well. Stir in tomatoes with juice and salsa. Cover; cook on LOW 5 to 6 hours or on HIGH 2½ to 3 hours, or until chicken is tender.

3. Turn **CROCK-POT®** slow cooker to HIGH; stir in beans. Cover; cook 5 to 10 minutes or until beans are heated through. Ladle into shallow bowls; serve with desired toppings.

Makes 4 servings

Roast Tomato-Basil Soup

2 cans (28 ounces each) peeled whole tomatoes, drained and 3 cups liquid reserved

2½ tablespoons packed dark brown sugar

1 medium onion, finely chopped

3 cups chicken broth

3 tablespoons tomato paste

¼ teaspoon ground allspice

1 can (5 ounces) evaporated milk

¼ cup shredded fresh basil (about 10 large leaves)

Salt and black pepper, to taste

1. Preheat oven to 450°F. Line baking sheet with foil; spray with nonstick cooking spray. Arrange tomatoes on foil in single layer. Sprinkle with brown sugar and top with onion. Bake about 25 to 30 minutes or until tomatoes look dry and light brown. Let tomatoes cool slightly; finely chop.

2. Place tomato mixture, 3 cups reserved liquid from tomatoes, broth, tomato paste and allspice in **CROCK-POT®** slow cooker. Mix well. Cover; cook on LOW 8 hours or on HIGH 4 hours.

3. Add evaporated milk and basil; season with salt and pepper. Cook on HIGH 30 minutes or until hot.

Makes 6 servings

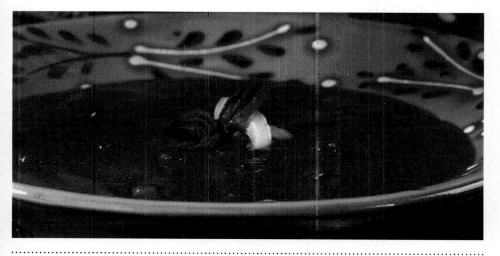

Parsnip and Carrot Soup

- 1 **medium leek, thinly sliced**
  Nonstick cooking spray
- 4 **medium parsnips, peeled and diced**
- 4 **medium carrots, peeled and diced**
- 4 **cups nonfat chicken broth or stock**
- 1 **bay leaf**

- ½ **teaspoon salt**
- ½ **teaspoon freshly ground pepper**
- ½ **cup small pasta, cooked al denté and drained**
- 1 **tablespoon chopped Italian parsley**
- 1 **cup low-fat croutons**

1. Cook leek in small nonstick skillet, sprayed with nonstick cooking spray, over medium heat until golden. Place in **CROCK-POT®** slow cooker.

2. Add parsnips, carrots, broth, bay leaf, salt and pepper. Cover; cook on LOW 6 to 9 hours or on HIGH 2 to 4 hours or until vegetables are tender. Add pasta during last hour of cooking.

3. Remove bay leaf. Sprinkle each individual serving with parsley and croutons.

Makes 4 servings

Note: This dish is a great year-round accompaniment to a main course of roasted meat. Or, the soup can stand alone as a quick, satisfying meal in its own right.

Tip: Recipe can be doubled for a 5-, 6- or 7-quart **CROCK-POT®** *slow cooker.*

Chicken and Sweet Potato Stew

4 boneless, skinless chicken breasts, cut into bite-size pieces

2 medium sweet potatoes, peeled and cubed

2 medium Yukon gold potatoes, peeled and cubed

2 medium carrots, peeled and cut into ½-inch slices

1 can (28 ounces) whole stewed tomatoes

1 teaspoon salt

1 teaspoon paprika

1 teaspoon celery seeds

½ teaspoon freshly ground black pepper

⅛ teaspoon ground cinnamon

⅛ teaspoon ground nutmeg

1 cup nonfat, low-sodium chicken broth

¼ cup fresh basil, chopped

1. Combine chicken, potatoes, carrots, tomatoes, salt, paprika, celery seeds, pepper, cinnamon, nutmeg and broth in **CROCK-POT**® slow cooker.

2. Cover; cook on LOW 6 to 8 hours or on HIGH 3 to 4 hours.

3. Sprinkle with basil just before serving.

Makes 6 servings

Note: This light stew has an Indian influence and offers excellent flavor without the fat.

Tip: Recipe can be doubled for a 5-, 6- or 7-quart CROCK-POT® slow cooker.

Golden Harvest Pork Stew

1 **pound boneless pork cutlets, cut into 1-inch pieces**

2 **tablespoons all-purpose flour, divided**

1 **tablespoon vegetable oil**

2 **medium Yukon gold potatoes, unpeeled and cut into 1-inch cubes**

1 **large sweet potato, peeled and cut into 1-inch cubes**

1 **cup chopped carrots**

1 **ear corn, broken into 4 pieces or ½ cup corn**

½ **cup chicken broth**

1 **jalapeño pepper, seeded and finely chopped***

1 **clove garlic, minced**

1 **teaspoon salt**

¼ **teaspoon black pepper**

¼ **teaspoon dried thyme**

Chopped parsley

*Jalapeño peppers can sting and irritate the skin, so wear rubber gloves when handling peppers and do not touch eyes.

1. Toss pork pieces with 1 tablespoon flour; set aside. Heat oil in large skillet over medium-high heat until hot. Add pork; cook until browned on all sides. Transfer to **CROCK-POT®** slow cooker.

2. Add remaining ingredients except parsley and 1 tablespoon flour. Cover; cook on LOW 5 to 6 hours.

3. Combine remaining 1 tablespoon flour and ¼ cup cooking liquid from stew in small bowl; stir until smooth. Stir flour mixture into stew. Cook on HIGH 10 minutes or until thickened. To serve, sprinkle with parsley.

Makes 4 servings

Creamy Cauliflower Bisque

1 pound frozen cauliflower florets

1 pound baking potatoes, peeled and cut into 1-inch cubes

1 cup chopped yellow onion

2 cans (about 14 ounces each) fat-free, reduced-sodium chicken broth

½ teaspoon dried thyme

¼ teaspoon garlic powder

⅛ teaspoon ground red pepper

1 cup evaporated skim milk

2 tablespoons butter

½ teaspoon salt

¼ teaspoon black pepper

1 cup (4 ounces) shredded reduced-fat sharp Cheddar cheese

¼ cup finely chopped parsley

¼ cup finely chopped green onion

1. Combine cauliflower, potatoes, onion, broth, thyme, garlic powder and ground red pepper in **CROCK-POT**® slow cooker. Cover; cook on LOW 8 hours, or on HIGH 4 hours.

2. Pour soup in blender in batches; process until smooth, holding lid down firmly. Return puréed batches to slow cooker. Add milk, butter, salt and black pepper; stir until blended.

3. Top individual servings with cheese, parsley and green onions.

Makes 9 servings

sides

Corn on the Cob
with Garlic Herb Butter

½ cup (1 stick) unsalted butter, at room temperature

3 to 4 cloves garlic, minced

2 tablespoons finely minced fresh parsley

4 to 5 ears of corn, husked

Salt and freshly ground black pepper, to taste

1. Thoroughly mix butter, garlic and parsley in small bowl.

2. Place each ear of corn on a piece of aluminum foil and generously spread butter on each ear. Season corn with salt and pepper and tightly seal foil. Place corn in **CROCK-POT®** slow cooker; overlap ears, if necessary. Add enough water to come one fourth of the way up each ear.

3. Cover; cook on LOW 4 to 5 hours or on HIGH 2 to 2½ hours or until done.

Makes 4 to 5 servings

Herbed Fall Vegetables

2 medium Yukon gold potatoes, peeled and cut into ½-inch dice

2 medium sweet potatoes, peeled and cut into ½-inch dice

3 parsnips, peeled and cut into ½-inch dice

1 medium head of fennel, sliced and cut into ½-inch dice

½ to ¾ cup chopped fresh herbs, such as tarragon, parsley, sage or thyme

4 tablespoons (½ stick) butter, cut into small pieces

1 cup chicken broth

1 tablespoon Dijon mustard

1 tablespoon salt

Freshly ground black pepper, to taste

1. Combine potatoes, parsnips, fennel, herbs and butter in **CROCK-POT®** slow cooker.

2. Whisk together broth, mustard, salt and pepper in small bowl. Pour mixture over vegetables. Cover; cook on LOW 4½ hours or on HIGH 3 hours or until vegetables are tender, stirring occasionally to ensure even cooking.

Makes 6 servings

Broccoli and Cheese Strata

2 cups chopped broccoli florets

4 slices firm white bread, ½-inch thick

4 teaspoons butter

1½ cups (6 ounces) shredded Cheddar cheese

1½ cups low-fat (1%) milk

3 eggs

½ teaspoon salt

½ teaspoon hot pepper sauce

⅛ teaspoon black pepper

1. Butter 1-quart casserole or soufflé dish that will fit in **CROCK-POT®** slow cooker. Cook broccoli in boiling water 10 minutes or until tender. Drain. Spread 1 side of each bread slice with 1 teaspoon butter. Arrange 2 slices bread, buttered sides up, in prepared casserole dish. Layer cheese, broccoli and remaining 2 bread slices, buttered sides down.

2. Beat milk, eggs, salt, hot sauce and black pepper in medium bowl. Slowly pour over bread.

3. Place small wire rack in **CROCK-POT®** slow cooker. Pour in 1 cup water. Place casserole on rack. Cover; cook on HIGH 3 hours.

Makes 4 servings

Scalloped Potatoes and Parsnips

6 **tablespoons unsalted butter**	2 **baking potatoes, cut in half lengthwise, then crosswise into ¼-inch slices**
3 **tablespoons all-purpose flour**	
1¾ **cups whipping cream**	2 **parsnips, cut into ¼-inch slices**
2 **teaspoons dry mustard**	1 **onion, chopped**
1½ **teaspoons salt**	2 **cups (8 ounces) shredded sharp Cheddar cheese**
1 **teaspoon dried thyme**	
½ **teaspoon black pepper**	

1. To prepare cream sauce, melt butter in medium saucepan over medium-high heat. Whisk in flour; cook 1 to 2 minutes. Slowly whisk in cream, mustard, salt, thyme and pepper until smooth.

2. Place potatoes, parsnips and onion in **CROCK-POT®** slow cooker. Add cream sauce. Cover; cook on LOW 7 hours or on HIGH 3½ hours or until potatoes are tender.

3. Stir in cheese. Cover; let stand until cheese melts.

Makes 4 to 6 servings

Spicy Beans Tex-Mex

⅓ cup lentils

1⅓ cups water

5 strips bacon

1 onion, chopped

1 can (15 ounces) pinto beans, rinsed and drained

1 can (15 ounces) red kidney beans, rinsed and drained

1 can (14½ ounces) diced tomatoes, undrained

3 tablespoons ketchup

3 cloves garlic, minced

1 teaspoon chili powder

½ teaspoon ground cumin

¼ teaspoon red pepper flakes

1 bay leaf

1. Combine lentils and water in large saucepan. Boil 20 to 30 minutes; drain.

2. Cook bacon in medium skillet until crisp. Transfer to paper towels to drain. Cool, then crumble bacon. In same skillet, cook onion in bacon drippings until tender.

3. Combine lentils, bacon, onion, beans, tomatoes with juice, ketchup, garlic, chili powder, cumin, pepper flakes and bay leaf in **CROCK-POT**® slow cooker. Cover; cook on LOW 5 to 6 hours or on HIGH 3 to 4 hours. Remove bay leaf before serving.

Makes 8 to 10 servings

Deluxe Potato Casserole

1 **can (10³/₄ ounces) condensed cream of chicken soup, undiluted**

1 **container (8 ounces) sour cream**

¼ **cup chopped onion**

¼ **cup plus 3 tablespoons melted butter, divided**

1 **teaspoon salt**

2 **pounds red potatoes, peeled and diced**

2 **cups (8 ounces) shredded Cheddar cheese**

1½ **to 2 cups stuffing mix**

1. Combine soup, sour cream, onion, ¼ cup butter and salt in small bowl.

2. Combine potatoes and cheese in **CROCK-POT**® slow cooker. Pour soup mixture over potato mixture; mix well. Sprinkle stuffing mix over potato mixture; drizzle with remaining 3 tablespoons butter. Cover; cook on LOW 8 to 10 hours or on HIGH 5 to 6 hours, or until potatoes are tender.

Makes 8 to 10 servings

Risotto-Style Peppered Rice

1 cup uncooked converted long-grain rice

1 medium green bell pepper, chopped

1 medium red bell pepper, chopped

1 cup chopped onion

½ teaspoon ground turmeric

⅛ teaspoon ground red pepper (optional)

1 can (14½ ounces) fat-free chicken broth

4 ounces Monterey Jack cheese with jalapeño peppers, cubed

½ cup milk

4 tablespoons (½ stick) butter, cut into small pieces

1 teaspoon salt

1. Place rice, bell peppers, onion, turmeric and ground red pepper, if desired, in **CROCK-POT®** slow cooker. Stir in broth. Cover; cook on LOW 4 to 5 hours or until rice is tender and broth is absorbed.

2. Stir in cheese, milk, butter and salt; fluff rice with fork. Cover; cook on LOW 5 minutes or until cheese melts.

Makes 4 to 6 servings

Tip: Dairy products should be added at the end of the cooking time because they could curdle if cooked in the CROCK-POT® slow cooker for a long time.

Winter Squash and Apples

1 teaspoon salt	2 apples, cored and cut into slices
½ teaspoon black pepper	1 medium onion, quartered and sliced
1 butternut squash (about 2 pounds), peeled and seeded	1½ tablespoons butter

1. Combine salt and pepper in small bowl; set aside.

2. Cut squash into 2-inch pieces; place in **CROCK-POT**® slow cooker. Add apples and onion. Sprinkle with salt mixture; stir well. Cover; cook on LOW 6 to 7 hours or until vegetables are tender.

3. Just before serving, stir in butter and season to taste with additional salt and pepper.

Makes 4 to 6 servings

Spanish Paella-Style Rice

2 cans (14½ ounces each) chicken broth

1½ cups uncooked converted long-grain rice

1 small red bell pepper, diced

⅓ cup dry white wine or water

½ teaspoon saffron threads, crushed or ½ teaspoon ground turmeric

⅛ teaspoon red pepper flakes

½ cup frozen peas, thawed

Salt, to taste

1. Combine broth, rice, bell pepper, wine, saffron and red pepper flakes in **CROCK-POT®** slow cooker; mix well. Cover; cook on LOW 4 hours or until liquid is absorbed.

2. Stir in peas. Cover; cook 15 to 30 minutes or until peas are hot. Season with salt.

Makes 6 servings

Tip: Paella can contain a variety of meats as well. For more authenticity— and to turn this dish into a delicious main course—add ½ cup cooked ham, chicken, chorizo or seafood when you add the peas.

Cornbread and Bean Casserole

Filling
- 1 **medium onion, chopped**
- 1 **medium green bell pepper, diced**
- 2 **cloves garlic, minced**
- 1 **can (16 ounces) red kidney beans, rinsed and drained**
- 1 **can (16 ounces) pinto beans, rinsed and drained**
- 1 **can (16 ounces) diced tomatoes with green chilies, undrained**
- 1 **can (8 ounces) tomato sauce**
- 1 **teaspoon chili powder**
- ½ **teaspoon ground cumin**
- ½ **teaspoon black pepper**
- ¼ **teaspoon hot pepper sauce**

Topping
- 1 **cup yellow cornmeal**
- 1 **cup all-purpose flour**
- 2½ **teaspoons baking powder**
- 1 **tablespoon sugar**
- ½ **teaspoon salt**
- 1¼ **cups milk**
- 2 **eggs**
- 3 **tablespoons vegetable oil**
- 1 **can (8½ ounces) cream-style corn, undrained**

1. For Filling: spray **CROCK-POT®** slow cooker with nonstick cooking spray. Cook onion, bell pepper and garlic in large skillet over medium heat until tender. Transfer to **CROCK-POT®** slow cooker.

2. Stir in beans, tomatoes with juice, tomato sauce, chili powder, cumin, black pepper and hot sauce. Cover; cook on HIGH 1 hour.

3. For Topping: combine cornmeal, flour, baking powder, sugar and salt in large bowl. Stir in milk, eggs and oil; mix well. Stir in corn. Spoon evenly over bean mixture in **CROCK-POT®** slow cooker. Cover; cook on HIGH 1½ to 2 hours or until cornbread topping is done.

Makes 6 to 8 servings

Tip: Spoon any remaining cornbread topping into greased muffin cups; bake 30 minutes at 375°F or until golden brown.

Orange-Spice Glazed Carrots

1 package (32 ounces) baby carrots

½ cup packed light brown sugar

½ cup orange juice

3 tablespoons butter or margarine

¾ teaspoon ground cinnamon

¼ teaspoon ground nutmeg

¼ cup cold water

2 tablespoons cornstarch

1. Combine carrots, sugar, orange juice, butter, cinnamon and nutmeg in **CROCK-POT®** slow cooker. Cover; cook on LOW 3½ to 4 hours or until carrots are crisp-tender.

2. Spoon carrots into serving bowl. Transfer cooking liquid to small saucepan. Bring to a boil.

3. Mix water and cornstarch until smooth; stir into saucepan. Boil 1 minute or until thickened, stirring constantly. Spoon over carrots.

Makes 6 servings

sweets

Bananas Foster

12 bananas, cut into quarters

1 cup flaked coconut

1 teaspoon ground cinnamon

½ teaspoon salt

1 cup dark corn syrup

⅔ cup butter, melted

2 teaspoons grated lemon peel

¼ cup lemon juice

2 teaspoons rum

12 slices pound cake

1 quart vanilla ice cream

Combine bananas and coconut in **CROCK-POT**® slow cooker. Combine cinnamon, salt, corn syrup, butter, lemon peel, lemon juice and rum in medium bowl; pour over bananas. Cover; cook on LOW 1 to 2 hours. To serve, arrange bananas on pound cake slices. Top with ice cream and pour on warm sauce.

Makes 12 servings

Hot Fudge Cake

1¾ cups packed light brown sugar, divided

2 cups all-purpose flour

¼ cup plus 3 tablespoons unsweetened cocoa powder, divided, plus additional for dusting, if desired

2 teaspoons baking powder

1 teaspoon salt

1 cup milk

4 tablespoons (½ stick) butter, melted

1 teaspoon vanilla

3½ cups boiling water

1. Coat 4½-quart **CROCK-POT®** slow cooker with nonstick cooking spray or butter. Mix 1 cup sugar, flour, 3 tablespoons cocoa powder, baking powder and salt in medium bowl. Stir in milk, butter and vanilla. Mix until well-blended. Pour into **CROCK-POT®** slow cooker.

2. Blend remaining ¾ cup sugar and ¼ cup cocoa powder in small bowl. Sprinkle evenly over mixture in **CROCK-POT®** slow cooker. Pour in boiling water. Do not stir.

3. Cover; cook on HIGH 1¼ to 1½ hours or until toothpick inserted into center comes out clean. Allow cake to rest 10 minutes, then invert onto serving platter or scoop into serving dishes. Serve warm; dust with cocoa powder, if desired.

Makes 6 to 8 servings

Cherry Delight

1 can (21 ounces) cherry pie filling

1 package (18¼ ounces) yellow cake mix

½ cup (1 stick) butter, melted

⅓ cup chopped walnuts

Whipped topping or vanilla ice cream (optional)

Place pie filling in **CROCK-POT®** slow cooker. Mix together cake mix and butter in medium bowl. Spread evenly over cherry filling. Sprinkle walnuts on top. Cover; cook on LOW 3 to 4 hours or on HIGH 1½ to 2 hours. Spoon into serving dishes, and serve warm with whipped topping or ice cream, if desired.

Makes 8 to 10 servings

Homestyle Apple Brown Betty

6 cups of your favorite cooking apples, peeled, cored and cut into eighths

1 cup bread crumbs

1 teaspoon ground cinnamon

1 teaspoon ground nutmeg

⅛ teaspoon salt

¾ cup packed brown sugar

½ cup (1 stick) butter or margarine, melted

¼ cup finely chopped walnuts

1. Lightly grease **CROCK-POT®** slow cooker. Place apples in bottom.

2. Combine bread crumbs, cinnamon, nutmeg, salt, brown sugar, butter and walnuts, and spread over apples.

3. Cover; cook on LOW 3 to 4 hours or on HIGH 2 hours.

Makes 8 servings

Note: This recipe conjures up an amazing dessert out of simple ingredients.

Tip: Recipe can be doubled for a 5-, 6- or 7-quart **CROCK-POT®** *slow cooker.*

Banana Nut Bread

⅓ cup butter or margarine

⅔ cup sugar

2 eggs, well beaten

2 tablespoons dark corn syrup

3 ripe bananas, well mashed

1¾ cups all-purpose flour

2 teaspoons baking powder

½ teaspoon salt

¼ teaspoon baking soda

½ cup chopped walnuts

1. Grease and flour inside of **CROCK-POT**® slow cooker. Cream butter in large bowl with electric mixer until fluffy. Slowly add sugar, eggs, corn syrup and mashed bananas. Beat until smooth.

2. Sift together flour, baking powder, salt and baking soda in small bowl. Slowly beat flour mixture into creamed mixture. Add walnuts and mix thoroughly. Pour into **CROCK-POT**® slow cooker. Cover; cook on HIGH 2 to 3 hours.

3. Let cool, then turn bread out onto serving platter.

Makes 6 servings

Note: Banana nut bread has always been a favorite way to use up those overripe bananas. Not only is it delicious, but it also freezes well for future use.

*Tip: Recipe can be doubled for a 5-, 6- or 7-quart **CROCK-POT**® slow cooker.*

Peanut Fudge Pudding Cake

1 **cup all-purpose flour**
1 **cup sugar, divided**
1½ **teaspoons baking powder**
⅔ **cup milk**
2 **tablespoons vegetable oil**
1 **teaspoon vanilla**

½ **cup peanut butter**
¼ **cup unsweetened cocoa powder**
1 **cup boiling water**
   Chopped peanuts (optional)
   Vanilla ice cream (optional)

1. Coat 4½-quart **CROCK-POT®** slow cooker with nonstick cooking spray or butter. Combine flour, ½ cup sugar and baking powder in medium bowl. Add milk, oil, vanilla and peanut butter. Mix until well blended. Pour batter into **CROCK-POT®** slow cooker.

2. Combine remaining ½ cup sugar and cocoa in small bowl. Stir in water. Pour into prepared **CROCK-POT®** slow cooker. Do not stir.

3. Cover; cook on HIGH 1¼ to 1½ hours or until toothpick inserted into center comes out clean. Allow cake to rest 10 minutes, then scoop into serving dishes or invert onto serving platter. Serve warm with chopped peanuts and ice cream, if desired.

Makes 4 servings

*Tip: Because this recipe makes its own fudge topping, be sure to spoon some of it from the bottom of the **CROCK-POT®** slow cooker when serving, or invert the cake for a luscious chocolately finish.*

Fresh Berry Compote

2 **cups fresh blueberries**

4 **cups fresh sliced strawberries**

2 **tablespoons orange juice**

½ **to ¾ cup sugar**

4 **slices (½ × 1½ inches) lemon peel with no white pith**

1 **cinnamon stick or ½ teaspoon ground cinnamon**

1. Place blueberries in **CROCK-POT®** slow cooker. Cover; cook on HIGH 45 minutes until blueberries begin to soften.

2. Add strawberries, orange juice, ½ cup sugar, lemon peel and cinnamon stick. Stir to blend. Cover; cook on HIGH 1 to 1½ hours or until berries soften and sugar dissolves. Check for sweetness and add more sugar if necessary, cooking until added sugar dissolves.

3. Transfer **CROCK-POT®** slow cooker to heatproof surface and let cool. Serve compote warm or chilled.

Makes 4 servings

Tip: To turn this compote into a fresh-fruit topping for cake, ice cream, waffles or pancakes, carefully spoon out fruit, leaving cooking liquid in **CROCK-POT®** *slow cooker. Blend 1 to 2 tablespoons cornstarch with ¼ cup cold water until smooth. Add to cooking liquid and cook on HIGH until thickened. Return fruit to sauce and blend in gently.*

index

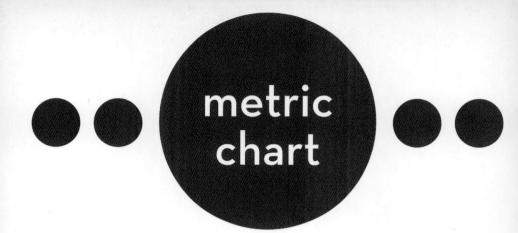

metric chart

VOLUME MEASUREMENTS (dry)

¹/₈ teaspoon = 0.5 mL
¹/₄ teaspoon = 1 mL
¹/₂ teaspoon = 2 mL
³/₄ teaspoon = 4 mL
1 teaspoon = 5 mL
1 tablespoon = 15 mL
2 tablespoons = 30 mL
¹/₄ cup = 60 mL
¹/₃ cup = 75 mL
¹/₂ cup = 125 mL
²/₃ cup = 150 mL
³/₄ cup = 175 mL
1 cup = 250 mL
2 cups = 1 pint = 500 mL
3 cups = 750 mL
4 cups = 1 quart = 1 L

VOLUME MEASUREMENTS (fluid)

1 fluid ounce (2 tablespoons) = 30 mL
4 fluid ounces (¹/₂ cup) = 125 mL
8 fluid ounces (1 cup) = 250 mL
12 fluid ounces (1¹/₂ cups) = 375 mL
16 fluid ounces (2 cups) = 500 mL

WEIGHTS (mass)

¹/₂ ounce = 15 g
1 ounce = 30 g
3 ounces = 90 g
4 ounces = 120 g
8 ounces = 225 g
10 ounces = 285 g
12 ounces = 360 g
16 ounces = 1 pound = 450 g

DIMENSIONS

¹/₁₆ inch = 2 mm
¹/₈ inch = 3 mm
¹/₄ inch = 6 mm
¹/₂ inch = 1.5 cm
³/₄ inch = 2 cm
1 inch = 2.5 cm

OVEN TEMPERATURES

250°F = 120°C
275°F = 140°C
300°F = 150°C
325°F = 160°C
350°F = 180°C
375°F = 190°C
400°F = 200°C
425°F = 220°C
450°F = 230°C

BAKING PAN AND DISH EQUIVALENTS

Utensil	Size in Inches	Size in Centimeters	Volume	Metric Volume
Baking or Cake Pan (square or rectangular)	8×8×2	20×20×5	8 cups	2 L
	9×9×2	23×23×5	10 cups	2.5 L
	13×9×2	33×23×5	12 cups	3 L
Loaf Pan	8½×4½×2½	21×11×6	6 cups	1.5 L
	9×9×3	23×13×7	8 cups	2 L
Round Layer Cake Pan	8×1½	20×4	4 cups	1 L
	9×1½	23×4	5 cups	1.25 L
Pie Plate	8×1½	20×4	4 cups	1 L
	9×1½	23×4	5 cups	1.25 L
Baking Dish or Casserole			1 quart/4 cups	1 L
			1½ quart/6 cups	1.5 L
			2 quart/8 cups	2 L
			3 quart/12 cups	3 L